Silhouettes in the Garden

Uncovering Who You Were Meant to Be

by Lula Starling

This is a work of creative nonfiction. Names, identifying characteristics, and events may have been changed or reimagined for literary purposes.

For permissions, inquiries, or more information, contact:

LulaStarling@brinixholdings.com

Cover and interior design by Lula Starling. Printed in the United States of America.

ISBN:979-8-9997603-2-6

Acknowledgments

To my sons — thank you for being the quiet light in the fog. You are not the reason I

began healing, but you are the reason I kept going. Your existence reminds me every day

that a new story can always be written, and that love—even after pain—can still grow

into something whole and true.

This book is also for every reader who has felt unseen, unheard, or shaped by someone

else's script. I hope these pages give you permission to become who you were always

meant to be.

Table of Contents

Section II: Shadows and Silhouettes

The emotional weight of what was hidden, expected, or endured — being seen yet not

seen.

Section III: Reclamation

Where the shift begins — pulling your power back, refusing to play along, choosing self

over cycle.

Section IV: Merge It

The integration — growth, peace, presence, and the decision to no longer be fragmented.

Preface: Behind Silhouettes in the Garden

Silhouettes in the Garden: Uncovering Who You Were Meant to Be

by Lula Starling

There are stories that live in silence—passed down in glances, habits, and the spaces

between words. This book began not with a plan, but with a need. A need to breathe. A

need to speak what had long gone unspoken. A need to uncover the layers when I

couldn't yet see clearly what lay beneath.

The day I began writing this book—and working toward my true purpose—I felt hidden.

Not poetically hidden, but deeply buried under expectations, roles, and a routine that felt

like mud, obscuring who I truly was. I didn't know exactly how to remove those layers,

but I knew I had to start writing. Writing became my gentle excavation, my quiet

rebellion, my message to the world that I was finally ready to emerge from the shadows.

Silhouettes in the Garden is more than just a title; it's a symbol of the hidden identities

we all carry—partially visible, often unseen, always waiting patiently to be revealed. It's

the truth many of us experience—how we can be fully present yet feel unseen, how we

appear clearly defined while quietly struggling beneath.

These poems represent moments of memory, womanhood, and generational

wisdom—truths hidden beneath expectations and traditions. Some poems reflect who

others thought I should become; others speak clearly of the person I've discovered I was

always meant to be.

I wrote this collection to honor my great-grandmother, Lula Beatrice, whose legacy

encouraged me to uncover my authentic self. I wrote it for every soul who feels invisible,

covered, or bound by life's demands. And most importantly, I wrote it as a testament to

the freedom and joy found in uncovering who we truly are.

May these words guide you to gently remove what obscures you, revealing the radiant

silhouette of who you've always been meant to become.

— Lula Starling

Roots and Early Observations

The Name in Letters

She took their names, twisted, turned, Like magnets shifting, letters churned. A game of

sounds, a puzzle bright, A name created, stitched in light.

She swore it was hers, a name of design, Yet somehow, I'd hear it in voices not mine. For

all through the years, in places unknown,

I met reflections of the name I'd been shown.

A name unique, yet never alone,

A melody echoed, a rhythm well-known. A whisper carried, a sound set free- Yet none

quite owned it the way it owned me.

But Nikki? That name was not on the wall,

Not in the letters, not written at all. Not carved from the mix of what once was theirs,

But borrowed instead from an old soul's prayers.

A man named Nicholas, lost to the night, His story fading in tail lights bright. Gone in an instant, a life torn apart, Yet stitched to my name, as if in the dark.

And on the night when spirits rise, When masks are worn and shadows lie, I took my

first breath, as he took his last, A crossing of souls, the future, the past.

Did they know what they did? Did they sense the unseen?

That naming me Nikki was more than routine?

A thread of the lost, a whisper of fate,

A child of letters, yet bound to a date.

So now when they call me, I carry the sound,

A name from the living, a name from the ground.

And though I was given the letters anew,

I wonder sometimes-who answered who?

Old Lady Eyes

They called me an old soul before I could speak,

A child with a gaze both quiet and deep. Not just wisdom beyond my years, But

something timeless, something clear.

Born of roots that ran so wide,

Where elders walked and did not hide.

I saw the truths they tried to feign, The cracks behind the smiles they gave.

I saw through masks, through whispered deceit,

Through secrets buried, through wounds they repeat.

The liars, the thieves, the fools in disguise, Could never outmaneuver these old lady eyes.

The world made sense when none said it should,

I knew what was right when no one else could.

Too young to lead, too wise to ignore,

A child with a burden the past had in store.

Not just a daughter, not just a child, But the reset, the reckoning, the fate reconciled.

Yet what child should bear what time could not fix?

What soul should be given a path forged of bricks?

Still, here I stand, the past in my hands, Holding the thread, reweaving the strands.

Charles Street Days

A concrete space on Charles Street's line, Where days felt endless, warm, and kind. My

mother worked, the nights ran late, So I stayed with hands that shaped my fate.

She called her friend a cousin's name, Though blood or bond-both felt the same.

Skipping streets, the echoes played, In laughter's light, no debts were paid.

The park was ours, the court alive, With bouncing echoes, hopes would thrive.

We didn't count the things we lacked, Just ran ahead, no looking back.

Great-Grandfather, steadfast, true,

Came bearing bread and milk anew. A quiet love, a silent gift,

To keep us whole, to help us lift.

And when the days would stretch too long, I found my place where I belonged. By

Great-Grandmother's knowing side, Where laundry swayed and time stood wide.

The sheets, they whispered in the breeze, Soft in summer, crisp in freeze.

She let me help, small hands at play, Teaching love in her own way.

A shepherd watched, his eyes so keen, A guardian still and strong between The world

outside and where I'd lay, A friend I'd pet each passing day.

These moments stitched like cloth in sun,

A childhood woven, thread by one. No riches poured, no treasures fine, Just love that

stood the test of time.

The Man at the Gate

He came to the yard, but never inside, A visitor held at the edge of the tide. The stoop was

our meeting, the steps our divide.

Between what was past and what still had to rise.

A blue Monte Carlo, sleek in the sun, With Starship scrawled as if ready to run. A

motorcycle roared, the wind in my hair, A fleeting adventure, a moment of air.

My mother beside me, young but grown, A girl now a mother, yet still not her own. Sent

to her grandmother, tucked out of sight,

A story repeated, a hush in the night.

And there by the window, steady and still,

Great-Grandfather sat with a watchful will.

A sentinel waiting, silent and keen, Guarding the echoes of what he had seen.

As a child, I noticed but never asked why, Why men stood distant, why love felt shy. But

now as a woman, the truth's clear as glass-

He watched to ensure the past wouldn't pass .

The Day the Old Man Left

They said he was mean, a storm, a stone, Yet to me, he was warmth, he was flesh, he was bone.

A child of the fields, a son of the past, A man built to endure, made never to ask.

When food lost its taste, when medicine stung,

They sent me to him, the small, knowing one.

A look, a word, and he'd set things right, A battle he'd pause, but not for the fight.

Then death came knocking, as death always does,

And they led me in, though I was still young.

I cried, I shattered, I broke in that place,

And vowed never more to stand at death's face.

But grief would not listen, nor time let me be,

And sorrow took hold, too heavy for me. I wailed, I trembled, my chest caving in, Until

strong hands had to carry me then.

Out of the church, out of the pain, Away from the weight of loss uncontained. Too young

to hold it, too old not to know, That something once steady had faded below.

Some say he was a hundred or more, But years were lost in fires before. What I do know,

what still remains, Is I felt his loss like blood in my veins.

The Sunshine Truck

She was small, but never weak,

Four-foot-eleven, but a force unique. A woman bound by time's cruel thread, Yet fire still burned where others bled.

I once saw tears slip down her face, Silent sorrow, soft disgrace.

But the next I knew, her hands held tight, A cast iron skillet, raised for flight.

Through the back door, he ran, he fled, With footsteps echoing words unsaid. A tiny

woman, fists of steel,

Chasing ghosts she'd long concealed.

On payday runs, I held her hand,

Through every stop in this small-town land. Bills paid in cash, a lollipop prize,

The world was warmth in people's eyes.

Then the drive-thru, the final stop, A pint of Carstairs, a silent drop.

The man would joke, she'd force a smile, A ritual traced in quiet denial.

Not for pleasure, not for cheer,

But to dull the truth she lived each year. A woman married, yet left alone,

Chasing a man who'd never come home.

"Look, there he go," she'd nod and say, Watching the past slip miles away. A parked car, a

truth unspoken,

A vow still whole, yet long since broken.

She drank, she watched, she held her place, Trapped in time she couldn't erase. But when

he passed, the drinking died, No more bottles, no more lies.

She married late, yet far too soon, And spent her years beneath the moon— Longing for

roads she'd never see, For skies too wide, for wings too free.

When the Men Came

She stood at the edge of her womanhood's door,

And the men, they gathered-some known, some lore.

Like shadows cast in the glow of her light, Drawn to her laughter, drawn to her sight.

One man, kind, with hands that stayed, A quiet love in the gifts he laid.

A second toe, a mirrored sign,

A Christmas spent, a dream aligned.

He built my world with plastic and glue, Barbie's castle, pink and new.

I wished for love, I wished for time, But wishes fade, and so did mine.

For just as he came, he slipped away, A whisper lost in yesterday.

And in his place, upon the court, Another man took up the sport.

The basketball bounced, the rhythm sure, A game well-played, a lure, a lure. He spoke in

tones both smooth and bright,

A shining thing in the dimming light.

But not all gold is meant to gleam, And not all men are what they seem. The court, the

game, the charm, the face, Would set our lives in splintered place.

Yet unlike those who came before, He did not leave-he stayed for more. His presence

grew, his voice held weight, And soon, he shaped the path of fate.

He did not drift, he did not fade, But in his staying, a price was paid.

For where I once stood by her side, A space grew wide, a shift, a tide.

The flicker sparked, the fracture spread, A love once whole, now left unsaid. And though

the house still held us tight, The air between no longer right.

For when the men came, one remained, And with him, all the lines were changed

The Sister That Wasn't

The years rolled by, yet stayed the same, The fights, the shouts, the whispered blame.

The bottle clinked, the doors slammed tight, Chaos ruled our home at night.

I shielded him, I played my part,

A child with armor, a guarded heart. Yet every storm that shook the walls, Left cracks too

deep, too wide, too tall.

Eleven moves in ten short years,

Boxes stacked with silent fears.

A home one day, a loss the next,

No roots to hold, just space to stretch.

And so I left—my sons in tow,

A promise made, a path to go.

I swore that they would never see, The life that had been given me.

But distance stretched, as distance does, Years passed by, a life was won.

Then home again, a visit brief,

And there he stood, still wrapped in grief.

"You left me there, you walked away," His voice held things I couldn't say. Memories

sharp where mine were dim, A past that never loosened him.

"52 pickup," he spat the game,

A child's hurt, an old refrain.

Moments lost in time's cruel tide,

Yet held like wounds that never died.

I told him plain, I told him true,

"I was a child, just like you."

But truth does not erase the past, And hurt unhealed will always last.

Now silence lingers, space remains, Two souls once close, now estranged. For bonds not

built on rightful ground,

Will one day break, not bend, not bound.

The Shadow Beside the Cradle

They brought him home, wrapped soft and new, A bundle of light, of cries that grew.

The center of hands, the hush, the coo, The baby, the wonder—the world he drew.

I stood at the edge, eight years tall,

A child no longer, yet still too small.

I knew it was normal, the shift, the space, Yet something in me still felt out of place.

The voices swarmed, their laughter bright, They held him close, bathed in light. And I, in

the corner, silent, still,

Felt the air grow thick, felt the chill.

It wasn't the love—I knew that well,

It was something deeper, harder to tell. A whisper of past, a history tight,

The way skin shades could steal the light.

He bore my mother's golden hue,

While mine was deep, a darker view. And though we shared the same strong line, The world saw more in what wasn't mine.

They marveled at him, his perfect glow, Their hands reached out, their voices low. "So

fair, so sweet, look at his face!"

And I? I simply filled the space.

A shadow beside the cradle stood,

Knowing too well, too soon, too good. Not old enough to name the weight,

Yet old enough to taste its shape.

But love is tricky, time is wise,

And truth still lurks behind young eyes. For soon I'd stand, though still so small, To catch

him each time he'd start to fall.

A sister first, a mother next,

A bond entwined in love complex.

And though the past may whisper low,

I held him close—I let him know.

Not My Son

At first, he was hers, the center, the prize, A mother's joy in adoring eyes.

But love in our house was like shifting sand, Slipping too quick from an unsteady hand.

The fights would come, the voices would break,
Promises shattered, hearts left to ache.

And when night fell with echoes tight,

It was me who held him through the night.

Soft whispers hummed, my hands so small, Wiping his tears before they could fall. Not a

mother, not yet grown,

But in those moments, I was all he'd known.

By day, we wandered, shuffled, sent,

Pushed outside when the anger spent. Neighbors watched, their glances wide, A child too

tall with one at her side.

I walked the streets, the stroller swayed, Through roads where old ghosts never fade.

And one woman stared, her gaze too long, Her lips pursed tight, as if something was wrong.

Then finally she stopped, her voice came through,
Heavy with meaning, but words

askew. I don't recall what she meant to say,

Only the weight of that moment stayed.

But I knew, I knew, before she was done— She thought
my brother was my son.

"No," I told her, my voice was sure,

"This is my brother, nothing more."

But her eyes still lingered, doubtful, slow, Like she knew
some truth I didn't know.

She said no more, just turned away,

Left me there in that heavy gray.

And I, a child, just stood there still,

Feeling the weight I'd always feel.

A Child Should Not Chase

I came when the calendar circled the day, A holiday visit, a birthday display. Few and far,

yet never too far,

Still, I was the one who had to depart.

They'd greet me with smiles, then sigh and decree,

"You only come when it's Christmas or we

"Forget all about us, don't call, don't stay," As if I, a child, could lead the way.

Guilt draped in laughter, a casual sting, A weight too heavy for small hands to bring.

For wasn't it them, the ones grown and wise,

Who should have come seeking, with love in their eyes?

I walked as I walked-just feet on the ground,

But whispers still followed, circling 'round. "Swishing," she'd call it, a lesson to heed, As if

I commanded where gazes would lead.

I did not know, not then, not yet,

That girls bore burdens they'd never have met.

That steps could be questioned, that blame could be laid,

On feet still learning the paths to be made.

So I came when I could, and I left when I must,

Watched love weighed heavy with distance and dust.

And though I was small, I somehow still knew-

A child should not chase what won't reach for you.

Shadows and Silhouettes

No Allies

He stepped through the door he should never have crossed, A father in name, but the title was lost.

The nights held secrets, the walls knew my shame, And I learned too young that love wasn't the same.

But I spoke, I broke, I shattered the dark,

Told my truth, lit the spark.

And for a moment, the world did right,

Police were called, he vanished from sight.

Counseling came, a quiet space,

A chance to heal, to leave no trace.

But time is cruel, and struggle bends,

And misery makes the weak defend.

Groceries in hand, he stood once more,

A man the law forbade our door.

And she, my mother, turned to me,

With eyes that held no clarity.

"You see him now? You see his pain?
Are you sure, child? Would you say it again?"
And right then, I knew—clear as the sky,

That love is a lie when survival's the why.
That mothers can fail, that blood can betray,
That I was alone in every way.
So I made a vow to time itself,
To speed ahead, to free myself.
To run so far, to cut so clean,
That home would fade like a distant dream.
And now, she asks, her voice so light,
Like years erased the shattered night.
But silence stands where love should be,
And I owe no truths to her memory.

The Turning Point

I was not the child who clung or cried, Not the one who wished love denied. Men came

and went, their faces blurred, Yet none had left my spirit stirred.

One was kind, soft in his ways,

A man I wished had stayed those days. The other just a fleeting trace, No warning signs

upon his face.

But then came him-the man she chose,

The one who made the softness close. The air grew thick, the walls held tight, And I

watched love shift into fight.

Not words, not rage, not slamming doors, But bodies thrown to bruising floors. Fists that

spoke, that cracked, that tore, A love that wasn't love no more.

I was six, maybe seven then,

Too young for truth, too old to pretend. And though I couldn't name the wrong, I knew

this song-I knew this song.

For women before had walked this line, Had stood at altars, had crossed that time. Yet

why, oh why, when kindness knocked, Did she turn the key on doors long locked?

A choice was made, a path was set, A lesson carved in deep regret. And though I did not

hold the pen, I knew that night-I'd write my end.

A Dress I Didn't Choose

August heat pressed thick and slow, By the river where the waters flowed. Long Wharf

stood, a quiet stage, For vows that locked, for love engaged.

A flower girl in mint, not gold, A dress well-made, but stiff and cold. Puffed-up sleeves,

the ruffles grand, Yet none of this was what I planned.

The pictures hold what I forget, The dance, the smiles, the sun well-set. Yet even then, a

child so small,

I felt the weight, I heard the call.

The theme was set, the thread was spun, A life designed, yet not my own. For even as I

twirled that day,

I knew I'd wear the world their way.

Caged and Free

I was born on the cusp of a world torn in two,

Between what was fading and what was brand new.

Women once tethered to duties assigned, Now reaching for futures they dared to define.

They whispered advice from both sides of the line,

One voice said "be careful," the other "you're fine."

Some warned of the dangers of chasing too far,

Others just sighed at the weight of their scars.

I watched them in kitchens, in cradles, in doubt,

Their lives built on "musts," never voices raised loud.

They married, they mothered, they buried their dreams,

A life wrapped in silence, stitched up at the seams.

Great-Grandmother Lula, with eyes full of fire,

Tuned in to the worlds that she longed to acquire.

A ship in the stars, a grand house of gold, A prairie so endless, a story untold.

She sat there, escaping in scenes on a screen,

While duty and marriage erased what had been.

The youngest of many, the last in the chain,

Pressed into promises, bound into pain.

I see her now clearer than ever before, Not just as my elder, but someone who wore

The same silent hunger that lingers in me, A longing to wander, untethered and free.

I've done what was needed, I've followed the map,

Steady, responsible-no time to unwrap The dreams I once cradled, the whispers I hid,

Traded for checklists of all that I did.

But here at this threshold, the path turns anew,

The weight of the past, now slipping on through.

No longer beholden, no cage left to close, The wind calls my name, and this time—I'll go.

Reclamation

While You See Me, I'm Already Gone

You think you know me, standing here— But look again, I've disappeared.

A shadow moves, a silhouette,

A ghost of dreams you've never met.

For weeks, for months, for years I stayed, Enduring storms, my peace delayed. A steady

check, a safe routine—

A faded echo of my dream.

Yet something shifted, broke the chain, A whisper deep, refusing pain.

Realizing life is mine alone,

A destiny that's self-owned.

So quietly, I changed the plot,

Stopped fighting battles I had not

The will or wish to carry on,

My heart reclaimed, my spirit gone.

Now kindness comes, now smiles appear— But it's too late, my dear, my dear. The woman here is just a shell;

My soul has bid this place farewell.

While you see me, I'm already gone— My heart is free, my dreams are drawn. I chart my

course, I plot my flight,

Embracing hope, embracing light.

And women everywhere have known We leave inside long before we've shown. When

silence falls, and battles cease, Our hearts have claimed our quiet peace.

Life is not one endless road,

But adventures waiting to unfold.

Each step taken can change direction, Redefining our reflection.

So trust your soul, your inner guide, Your path is yours, your life to ride.

No path prescribed, no road foregone— They see you here, but you're already gone.

Almost (What Could Have Been)

You built up the moment, you gave it your heart— The dream felt so close, the perfect

new start. You pictured the future, each detail refined,

Every step planned, every path well-defined.

Then suddenly silence, or words gentle yet cold, A polite little rejection, "No," carefully told.

Left with questions unanswered, reasons unseen, Standing empty-handed in what might have been.

It's okay to feel wounded, to wonder and sigh, To replay the moments, asking yourself why.

Disappointment, a shadow, arrives unannounced, Shaking foundations, hopes firmly renounced.

Yet somewhere within it, beneath the lost chance, Lies something greater than mere

circumstance— Rejection's protection, redirecting your way,

Saving you quietly from some deeper dismay.

Still, let yourself linger in what almost became, Let heartache breathe softly, without guilt or shame. For grief over losses, opportunities missed,

Makes clearer the moments your soul truly wished.

And soon you will notice, when the ache fades and clears, That each "almost" was

needed to shift through your years. What felt like rejection, when seen looking back, Was

simply life's compass correcting your track.

So pause in the silence, feel the truth from within: It's alright to mourn softly what could

have been. For every closed door gently leads you toward grace, Guiding your steps to

your true rightful place.

Boundless

When we were small, we knew no bounds— Dreams were whispered, hopes profound.

Every path wide open, doors ajar;

We claimed the sky and chased each star.

Yet caution rose as years moved on, Words of doubt, belief withdrawn.

Warnings of limits, barriers set,

Echoes of dreams they'd never met.

They spoke their fears, their careful lines, Telling stories from their own confines. What

wasn't theirs, they said, wasn't mine; But destiny isn't theirs to define.

Today I choose, my vision clear— My dreams are louder than their fear. I'll move away, or

start anew;

Build a business, chase what's true.

Earn degrees and journeys bold,

Travel far, break every mold.

Decide my path, my time, my place, Stepping forward, owning space.

No voices matter more than these: The call ahead, the inner ease,

The truth I carry, the future bright— My road is clear, my path in sight.

I know I can, I hold my dream,

The life ahead is what I deem.

Ships cross oceans, planes take flight— Today, my turn to claim this right.

Boundaries vanish, fears dissolve; My story mine alone to solve.

I am worthy, strong, and true—

Today, I'll do what I must do.

Before me stretch these endless roads; No limits bind the dreams bestowed.

Each step forward sets me free— The world awaits the best of me.

Merge It

Why Can't Every Day Be Like This?

I took today to breathe and roam, No meetings, noise, or rush in sight.

Just wandered far from screens and home, To let my soul feel pure delight.

I ate my breakfast warm and slow, In Winter Haven's morning sun.

Where southern breezes softly blow, And life moves slow, not on the run.

The birds above began to sing, Their music sweeter than a tune.

I found downtown—a peaceful thing— With swings that danced beneath the moon.

I watched the people pass with grace, Each stranger held a spark, a glow. No frantic steps,

no hurried pace, Just kindness in the eyes they show.

It made me think—why not each day? Why chase and toil and lose our way? We buy and

spend, then work and pay, And trade our time for things that stay.

Though credit cards we may not touch, We still exchange our time for gold. We chase the

world's applause too much, And let our dearest dreams grow old.

But something in today felt clear— A whisper soft, a still, small voice. It told me, "Keep

your purpose near. You've always had the wiser choice."

To write my book, to build my brand, To pave a path both rich and true. To work for

joy—not just demand— And help inspire a chosen few.

So if this day has touched you too, Let it ignite your sleeping spark.

Begin again, start something new— Your dream still waits there in the dark.

The Fountain in the Square

I made my way through town today, Where farmers set their tables wide.

Fresh fruits and flowers on display, With joy and ease on every side.

The fountain in the square stood still, Its water clear beneath the light.

No festive hue, no painted thrill— Just simple beauty, calm and bright.

I sat beneath the southern sun,

Its golden light a soft embrace.

A quiet gift, a moment won, To pause amid life's hurried pace.

Two parents stood not far from me, Each child splashing in the stream. A girl, a boy—so

wild, so free—

As if the world became a dream.

The water danced, the laughter rang, Yet still, the city made no sound.

Though cars passed by and footsteps sang, A hush, like peace, hung all around.

It felt as if the earth stood still,

To let us feel what life could be.

A moment shaped not by our will, But by divine simplicity.

This fountain's spray, so cool, so light, Reminded me what matters most— A quiet day, a

sunbeam bright,

Not chasing things, not needing boast.

So here I sit and breathe and stay, While seasons rush and people part. I know I need

more days this way— With sunlit skies and a softened heart.

The Tales of Grimm and Shadow

Two cats, two fates, two stories untold, One bathed in sunlight, the other in coal. Both

found by chance, or maybe design, Two little souls that would soon become mine.

Grim, the Survivor

Once tossed from a car, left in the street, A life nearly ended before it could meet. But fate

had a way of bending the line, A stranger ran out, just in time.

She scooped him up, a bundle so small, Took him inside, away from it all.

A clinic, a checkup, a name to be claimed— "Grimm," she said, "for the Reaper he tamed."

Years later, with emerald eyes so wide, He strutted, he posed, a king in his stride. A ham,

a clown, a cat full of cheer,

Yet a warrior who'd conquered his fear. Shadow, the Wanderer

A rustling sound, a whisper, a glance,

A kitten too young to stand a chance.

Alone in the bushes, too tiny to roam,

Yet too wild at heart to call anywhere home.

I laid out food, I gave him a name,

But the streets had their rules, a cruel little game. The strays stole his meals, the fights

left him sore, So I opened my door... then I opened it more.

A bed of his own, a roof overhead,

A promise to help, no strings, no thread. A trip to the vet, a kindness, a plan—

But Shadow returned, as if he knew who I am. Two Stories, One Home

Now here we sit, in the house they both earned,

Two lives once broken, two souls that returned. One saved from the road, one saved from

the night, Both finding love in the gentlest light.

So perhaps there's a thread that binds what we save, A force, an intention, the paths that it paves. For all in my home have battled the storm, Yet still, they rise—whole and warm.

www.ingramcontent.com/pod-product-compliance
Lightning Source LLC
LaVergne TN
LVHW040221110826
845146LV00005B/1375

9798999760326